BIBLE 101

FIRST STEPS FOR
SPIRITUAL GROWTH

MIKE JOHNSON

ISBN-10: 0615969674
ISBN-13: 978-0615969671

Published by Start2Finish Books
PO Box 660675 #54705
Dallas, TX 75266-0675
www.start2finish.org

Printed in the United States of America

Unless otherwise noted, all Scripture quotations are from The Holy Bible, English Standard Version®, copyright © 2001 by Crossway Bibles, a publishing ministry of Good News Publishers. Used by permission. All rights reserved.

Cover Design: Josh Feit, Evangela.com

CONTENTS

1

BIBLE
AUTHORITY

You are a new Christian! You have obeyed the Gospel and your sins were taken away in the waters of baptism (Acts 2:38; 22:16). You were placed into Christ and into the family of God (Galatians 3:26-27). You were saved (Mark 16:15-16; 1 Peter 3:21). You obeyed the death, burial, and resurrection of Jesus (Romans 6:1-7).

Why did you do this? If you had done this in order to make someone in your family or a friend happy, you would have done it for the wrong reason. If you had done this because you were forced into it, you would have done it for the wrong reason. However, the reason you obeyed the Gospel is because you believe that the Bible is the Word of God and you did what you believed that Word to teach. It was your faith in God's Word that led you to obey the Gospel and be immersed for the forgiveness of your sins.

The subject of Bible authority is a basic foundational step as you begin your life as a Christian. There is a game we played as little children that was called, "Mother, may I?" The point of the game was to obtain permission to do something from the one who was playing the "Mother" role. Though my memory of the details of the game is somewhat fuzzy, the object of the one who was the "Mother" was to catch someone doing something without permission.

Finding out what pleases God and what He permits is the goal of proper Bible study. The only consistent approach to Bible authority is to seek God's permission for whatever action is under discussion. Therefore, the approach to Bible study in determining God's will concerning a given action is to ask the question, "God, may I...?"

This is a God-given, biblically-consistent concept. Paul wrote in Ephesians 5:10 that Christians should be busy trying "to discern what is pleasing to the Lord." Again, Paul wrote in 1 Thessalonians 5:21, "Test everything; hold fast what is good." These two verses make it clear that Christians must pursue and hold to those things that are pleasing (acceptable) to God. We do this by putting our questions to a test in order to find out what is acceptable to God.

The same Greek word is used in both verses, and is translated as "finding out" and "test". The word is *dokimazo*. This word is used in many other places in Scripture. Jesus used it in His parable of the wedding feast when one of the invited guests declined an invitation because he needed to "test" his five yoke of oxen (Luke 14:19). Luke 12:56 describes those who could "interpret the appearance of earth and sky." The word defines the work of fire that will "try" things put into it (1 Corinthians 3:13).

The Bible uses this word to challenge individuals to "examine" themselves (1 Corinthians 11:28; 2 Corinthians 13:5; Galatians 6:4), "prove what is good" (Romans 12:2), and "prove the sincerity of your love" (2 Corinthians 8:8). Furthermore, before a man is appointed as a deacon, he is to be "tested", (1 Timothy 3:10). The first-century Christians were instructed to "test the spirits to see whether they are from God" (1 John 4:1).

All of the words that translate the Greek word *dokimazo* call for a person to understand why he or she should take the action under consideration. In some way, a test must be used to prove or examine and, thereby, find out an answer. This is what discovering Bible authority is all about.

DEFINITION OF TERMS

The word "authority" means "the right to order or decide." The word "authorize" means "to permit officially." Whenever we speak, then, about Bible authority, we are saying that the Bible has the right to order or to decide the answers to our spiritual concerns. Therefore, authority is permission or license. A fishing license grants authority or permission to fish. A marriage license grants permission or authority for a couple to marry. Additionally, each license permits only the action for which it was given. You cannot use a fishing license to get married or a marriage license to fish.

Whatever the Bible authorizes, it permits or licenses. Whatever the Bible does not authorize, it does not permit or license. So, how does the Bible grant permission, give authority, or give license? The answers to this question reveal the style that God used to transmit His authority to those to whom He spoke in times past and to those who would read in the future.

GENERIC & SPECIFIC

Sometimes, the Bible authorizes generically and, sometimes, specifically. Generic authority concerns anything within a generic or general group. At other times, a more narrow or specific part of the larger group is under consideration. In this case, we find specific or limited authority. For example, a student may obtain generic permission from a teacher to be out of class and be wherever he wants to be. Most likely, however, a student will be given permission to be in a certain place. If the student obtains specific permission to be in the library, he has no permission to be in the gym or the lunchroom. However, if he merely obtains permission to be out of the classroom, then he has authority or license to be in any one of these places.

The same thing is true with the Word of God. When God told Noah to build an ark of "gopher wood" (Genesis 6:14), He specified what kind of wood to use. Noah was not free, then, to use any other kind of wood. Furthermore, God specifically told Noah, "the length of the ark 300 cubits, its breadth 50 cubits, and its height 30 cubits" (Genesis 6:15). Again, the ark should have three decks or floors, a window, and a door. Noah did not have permission or authority to change or leave out any one of these specific things that God told him.

However, God also gave him some generic authority. "Also take with you every sort of food that is eaten, and store it up. It shall serve as food for you and for them" (Genesis 6:21). God did not tell Noah what specific food to take on the ark with him. He was permitted to choose from all the available food what he would take on the ark.

This is exactly the way we deal with our children. When they are given permission or authority to go to Johnny's house, they do not have license to go to Suzie's house. However, if they are given permission to pick a friend's house to go to and then call when they get there, they have the right to choose among all their friends.

SILENT & SPOKEN

The second way that God's Word authorizes is through silence and statement. God rules authoritatively by what He does not say as well as by what He says. In Hebrews 7:14, this principle is plain. "For it is evident that our Lord arose from Judah, of which tribe Moses spoke nothing concerning priesthood." Aaron and his sons were appointed as priests between the people and God. This was "a perpetual priesthood throughout their generations" (Exodus 40:15). Aaron was of the tribe of Levi (Exodus 6:16-20). The tribe of Levi was the tribe from which all priests came. None came from any other tribe (Hebrews 7:13).

At the same time, the principle of silence operates. God spoke about the tribe of Levi as the priestly tribe. He spoke of no other tribe in that way. God's silence on the matter is just as authoritative as His speaking on the matter. It is just as authoritative that there could be no priests from another tribe as it was that the priests were to be appointed from the tribe of Levi.

EXPLICIT & IMPLICIT

The third way that God's Word authorizes is explicitly and implicitly. God's commands are examples of explicit statements. The implicit authority of God grows out of the explicit statements. Explicit statements leave no doubt, for they are clear and plain. No one disagrees over the clarity of an explicit statement, though they might disagree over its application. Explicit statements are just that—explicit!

Football coaches use explicit statements all the time. "Give me five laps, now!" Everyone on the team knows what he means when he says this. He means for the entire team to run five laps around the football field. There is nothing behind-the-scenes.

An implicit statement is more of a behind-the-scenes statement. It is not less authoritative; it is just not as forthright. We use implicit statements all the time, as well. A teacher might say, "Students, sit in your seats and I will be right back." Do you believe that any student has the authority to run around the room while the teacher is away? The obvious answer is, no. Though the teacher did not say explicitly to the students, "Stay in your seats," until she returned, they all should have understood what she was implying.

There are many explicit statements in the Bible. For example, Jesus used an explicit statement when He said in Matthew 28:19, "Go therefore and make disciples of all nations." This obvious explicit statement directed the apostles to go into every corner of the world to spread His message. We can be sure that this is also an explicit statement that was meant for us because Jesus continued, "teaching them to observe all that I have commanded you" (v. 20). Since Jesus commanded the apostles to preach the Gospel to all the world, and since He told them to teach all things that He taught them, then we, too, are to go into all the world and preach the Gospel.

There is also implicit authority within the explicit statement. There is implicit authority to "go into all the world" in any way that we choose. We are not limited in our going by an explicit statement requiring a certain means of travel.

These are the same ways that we use in every day life to authorize, permit, or give license to anyone to act. God also gives us His authority in the Bible in the same ways. God wrote the Bible in a way that we can understand it. God wants us to know His will. Therefore, let us understand what the will of the Lord is. When we understand, we have His authority.

Now, you might ask, "How did God write the Bible so that we can be sure we have His authority of our lives?" That question is the next one to consider.

GOD REVEALED THE BIBLE

Revelation refers to the origin of the Word of God. The Bible is a book that was revealed by God to those who wrote it down. Revelation, then, is the message that was given by God. To reveal something is to uncover and expose it. What God revealed could only be uncovered and exposed by God. It would not have been possible for anyone to research and to discover this message on his own.

Revelation originates in the mind of God and can be known outside of God's mind only when He chooses to reveal it. Romans 11:33 deals with this very theme. "Oh, the depth of the riches and wisdom and knowledge of God! How unsearchable are his judgments and how inscrutable his ways!"

When God chose to reveal what was in His mind, He revealed it to the Spirit. First Corinthians 2:11 states, "For who knows a person's thoughts except the spirit of that person, which is in him? So also no one comprehends the thoughts of God except the Spirit of God." In the same way that no one knows what is in the mind of any individual except that individual, no one knows what is in the mind of God except God.

GOD INSPIRED THE BIBLE

Inspiration refers to the delivery of the Word of God. As revelation is the message, inspiration is the method by which the revelation was written down. This term literally means "God-breathed". This word is used in 2 Timothy 3:16-17, "All Scripture is breathed out by God and profitable for teaching, for reproof, for correction, and for training in righteousness, that the man of God may be complete, equipped for every good work."

Inspiration is that process by which God enabled each writer to record accurately the revelation that he had been given. God not only provided the message to the writers, He also insured that they would write it down in the way that He wanted.

God used the Holy Spirit in this process. In 1 Corinthians 2:12-13, Paul declared the process by which he and others spoke God's Word. "Now we have received not the spirit of the world, but the

Spirit who is from God, that we might understand the things freely given us by God. And we impart this in words not taught by human wisdom but taught by the Spirit, interpreting spiritual truths to those who are spiritual."

Notice that God gave them the words to speak. He did not leave them alone to concoct the best terminology to say what God wanted. It would not make sense for God to do anything less than to be involved in the entire process that would insure the best words used to say just what God wanted to say.

But how did God do this? Second Peter 1:20-21 states, "knowing this first of all, that no prophecy of Scripture comes from someone's own interpretation. For no prophecy was ever produced by the will of man, but men spoke from God as they were carried along by the Holy Spirit." In some way, the Spirit of God so filled the writers that they recorded perfectly what God revealed. Furthermore, the Spirit so filled them that He picked from the storehouse of their minds the words that were most natural to each of them, but would also transmit the meaning that God intended in the best possible words. In this way, God provided the message and guided the method of writing it down so that it truly is the Word of God.

REVIEW QUESTIONS

1. What is the goal of Bible study?

2. Authority means...

3. Authorize means...

4. What are some synonyms for "authority"?

5. What are the three ways God wrote His authority into Scripture?

6. What is the definition of "revelation"?

7. Where does a revelation originate?

8. Who reveals the mind of God to us?

9. What is the definition of "inspiration"?

10. What is the literal meaning of "inspiration"?

11. Who/what compelled the writers of the Bible to write?

2.

OLD OR NEW TESTAMENT?

The Bible is really a book of 66 books. These books are divided into two main sections. The Old Testament has 39 books. The New Testament has 27 books. Various churches teach different things about the authority of these two main sections within the Bible.

Some teach that the Old Testament is still authoritative for daily living today. They follow many of the commands and rules in the Old Testament. It is their guide for living. Others teach that the Old Testament should be a guide for daily life along with the New Testament. The result is a hybrid religion that includes some things from the Old Testament and some things from the New Testament. But then there are those who teach that the Old Testament is no longer authoritative for daily living. The New Testament is God's guide for daily life today.

So, what is the right approach? Are the Old and New Testaments equally authoritative or does one stand in place of the other as a guide for daily living today?

TWO GROUPS OF PEOPLE

The Bible consistently refers to two groups of people in the world. All of the people of the world can be divided into these two groups. That is the basis of the Old Testament. "Therefore remember that at one time you Gentiles in the flesh, called 'the uncircumcision' by what is called the circumcision, which is made in the flesh by hands— remember that you were at that time separated from Christ, alienated from the commonwealth of Israel and strangers to the covenants of promise, having no hope and without God in the world" (Ephesians 2:11-12).

This text details the two divergent groups of people and reveals why there was such a tension between them. This passage was written to people who were Gentiles. Paul referred to them as the "uncircumcision." This was a fact. They did not practice circumcision. However, the Jews, who were the "circumcised," used the uncircumcision of the Gentiles as the main marker of their uncleanness. The Jews did not want to cross paths with Gentiles, lest that contact defile them.

The Jewish attitude toward the Gentiles caused two reactions. The Jews developed an attitude of arrogance that they were special before God and no one else was on their level of having the favor of God (at least that's how the Gentiles saw them—Acts 10:28). This attitude also produced within Gentiles a less-than-favorable attitude toward the things of God. If the Jews were examples of godly people, then they wanted nothing of it.

The truth is, though, that the Jews did have some advantages that the Gentiles did not have. Paul addressed this in Romans 3:1-2, "Then what advantage has the Jew? Or what is the value of circumcision? Much in every way. To begin with, the Jews were entrusted with the oracles of God." However, with these advantages came greater responsibility (Luke 12:48), and they failed miserably. They were not faithful to the word that God had given them. However, the

Gentiles were failures, too. They were guilty because "although they knew God, they did not honor him as God or give thanks to him" (Romans 1:21). They knew God through His creation (Romans 1:19-20). So Paul concludes in Romans 3:9, "What then? Are we Jews any better off? No, not at all. For we have already charged that all, both Jews and Greeks, are under sin." Ephesians 2:11-12 lists the differences between the Jews and the Gentiles supporting the assertions that the Jews had many advantages over the Gentiles.

The Gentiles were "separated from Christ." He did not come through the Gentile lineage. He was not "their" descendent. The Gentiles were "alienated from the commonwealth of Israel." They had no part in the special favor of God bestowed on the Jews. The Gentiles were "strangers to the covenants of promise." They had no part in the promises God had made to the Jews through the centuries. Because of these things, the Gentiles were without "hope and without God in the world." This is not an indictment that they were worse than the Jews. We have already discounted this.

However, it is true that they did not have the same access to God that the Jews enjoyed. It was the Old Testament law that showed the Jews who God was and how they could have a more intimate relationship with Him. While God revealed Himself generally to the Gentiles in the creation, He revealed Himself to the Jews specifically in written form—the Old Testament.

These two groups of people who spent centuries apart even hating each other, according to Paul, were now equal. This had always been true, though neither seemed to acknowledge it. "Is God the God of Jews only? Is he not the God of Gentiles also? Yes, of Gentiles also" (Romans 3:29).

THE TWO ARE ONE

Ephesians 2:13-18 develops this idea. The Gentiles who were far off have been brought near. "But now in Christ Jesus you who once were far off have been brought near by the blood of Christ" (v. 13). When Jesus shed His blood on the cross of Calvary, He closed the gap between the two groups of people. "For he himself is our peace, who has made us both one and has broken down in his flesh the dividing wall of hostility" (v. 14). Jesus closed the gap by removing that which effectively and actually divided the Jews from the Gentiles. The Jews were set apart as a separate people when God gave them the Law of Moses. That law guided their lives in every respect calling them out from the other nations.

"By abolishing the law of commandments expressed in ordinances, that he might create in himself one new man in place of the two, so making peace, and might reconcile us both to God in one body through the cross, thereby killing the hostility" (vv. 15-16). The text teaches that Jesus abolished the enmity. This is defined as "the law of commandments expressed in ordinances." What is Paul saying? Enmity is hatred. The Jews hated the Gentiles, and the Gentiles hated the Jews. Their hatred stemmed from the middle wall of separation. The Jews had a law and the Gentiles did not. So Jesus abolished that which separated them. To abolish means to "take it out of the way."

The law accomplished its purpose and was removed. Paul wrote in Galatians 3:19, "Why then the law? It was added because of transgressions, until the offspring should come to whom the promise had been made, and it was put in place through angels by an intermediary." Notice, that the law "was added because of transgressions." That is, the law was given after transgressions (sins) were already present. The law did not create sin; it revealed sin that was already present. The law was not a mistake or sinful in itself (Romans 7:7). The law of Moses revealed that people are sinful before God. Furthermore, the law demonstrated that no one can live perfectly before God. No law can make anyone perfect (Hebrews 10:1). The law was meant as a temporary thing (Galatians 3:24).

Jews and Gentiles now reside in one body. It was the cross of Jesus that created the possibility of unity between two groups of people who were totally at odds with each other. It was the purpose of the life of Jesus to reconcile these two groups to each other and to the God of the universe, before whom they both stood condemned because of their sin. "He came and preached peace to you who were far off and peace to those who were near" (Ephesians 2:17).

Paul, then, declares, "For through him we both have access in one Spirit to the Father" (Ephesians 2:18). This verse beautifully summarizes the entire heavenly plan that God put in motion from the beginning of time. After the sin of Adam and Eve in the Garden of Eden, the Lord God said to the serpent, "I will put enmity between you and the woman, and between your offspring and her offspring; he shall bruise your head, and you shall bruise his heel" (Genesis 3:15).

This Seed promise was extended to Abram when the Lord God promised that all people would be blessed by his Seed (Genesis 12:7). Galatians 3:16 identifies the Seed of that promise as Christ. Jesus was the "Seed" to Whom the entire Old Testament pointed. Furthermore, once that "Seed" had come, the Old Law had fulfilled its purpose and was ready to be taken away (Galatians 3:19). That Old Law was removed and another written word from the Lord given through the Spirit came into being.

Jesus promised His disciples that they would present the truth to the world following His departure, and the Spirit of God would guide them and give them all truth (John 16:13). This process is called "inspiration." God gave the truth to the writers of the New Testament through the agency of the Spirit who filled them as they wrote (2 Timothy 3:16-17).

Therefore, through Jesus' death and the Spirit's providing the truth of God, both Jews and Gentiles "have access...to the Father" (Ephesians 2:18). We live in the New Testament era. Today, God speaks to us through His word recorded in the New Testament. It is our guide for daily living. The Old Testament stands to teach us general principles about the nature of God and man. We should not overlook it (Romans 15:4).

REVIEW QUESTIONS

1. How many books are in the Bible?

The New Testament has _____ books.

The Old Testament has _____ books.

2. Into how many groups are people divided in the Bible?

3. How are they labeled?

4. What was wrong with the Jewish attitude?

5. What was wrong with the Gentile attitude?

6. The Jews sinned because:

7. The Gentiles sinned because:

8. The Jews had some spiritual advantages because the Gentiles were:

9. How have the two groups become one?

10. What was the wall of separation?

11. Why did God give the law of Moses to the Israelites?

12. Who was the "Seed" promised?

3

ESTABLISHMENT OF THE CHURCH

There are some who teach that the Church was an afterthought of God, following the rejection of Jesus by the Jews. Supposedly, God's plan was disrupted by the unbelieving Jews. He was then forced to set up an interim plan until He could establish the earthly kingdom that He had intended for Jesus to establish while He was on the earth.

There are at least two problems with this theory. The first one is that this view of history portrays God as being too inept or too weak to establish the earthly kingdom like He intended. Does it really make sense that the Jews or anyone else have the ability to thwart the ultimate plans of God? If God had said that He was going to have Jesus establish an earthly kingdom while He was on the earth, how could anyone disrupt that plan?

The second problem is that the Bible plainly states that the Church was in the eternal purpose of God. Ephesians 3:10-11 reads, "Through the church the manifold wisdom of God might now be made known to the rulers and authorities in the heavenly places. This was according to the eternal purpose that he has realized in Christ

Jesus our Lord." These verses teach two things. First, the Church was in the eternal purpose of God. Second, God accomplished what He set out to do in Christ Jesus.

The Church is not an afterthought of God. It was not a substitute for an earthly kingdom that was rejected by the Jews of Jesus' day. It was eternally purposed to exist. It was established in conjunction with the ministry of Jesus while He was on the earth.

OLD TESTAMENT PROPHESIED THE CHURCH WOULD BE ESTABLISHED

Isaiah 2:2-3 foresaw the establishment of the Church hundreds of years before it actually occurred. "It shall come to pass in the latter days that the mountain of the house of the LORD shall be established as the highest of the mountains, and shall be lifted up above the hills; and all the nations shall flow to it, and many peoples shall come, and say: 'Come, let us go up to the mountain of the LORD, to the house of the God of Jacob, that he may teach us his ways and that we may walk in his paths.' For out of Zion shall go the law, and the word of the LORD from Jerusalem."

THE TIME FACTOR

Notice the time frame of the events of this text. These things were going to happen "in the latter days." When did the latter days begin? They certainly began some time after the time of the writing of the prophecy. This text was looking forward to a time when these things would occur. It was not referring to anything happening during the time of the one who was speaking.

Hebrews 1:1-2 helps us with this: "Long ago, at many times and in many ways, God spoke to our fathers by the prophets, but in these last days he has spoken to us by his Son." These verses identify two time periods. One was a time when God spoke to the fathers through prophets. The fathers are obviously the ancestors of the Jewish people. God spoke to them by the use of prophets sent among them. However, the second time period is the one in which the author of the passage was living. He said that God "has spoken to us by his Son." He identified the time as "these last days."

The "latter days" in the Isaiah passage and the "last days" in the Hebrews passage are the same days. Since Isaiah identified a time called the "latter days," it is clear that he was living in the former days. The writer of Hebrews was living, not only in the "latter days," but he was also living in the "last days." That is, there is coming no other time period wherein God will speak to anyone in a different way. He spoke to the fathers by the prophets, and now He speaks "in the last days" by His Son. Therefore, Isaiah was looking forward to the time period when God spoke through His Son.

THE ACTION

Isaiah prophesied that, in the latter days, the Lord's house would be established. At the time of Isaiah's prophecy, the Jews were the people of God. Yet, he prophesied that there was coming a time when the Lord's house would be established. Therefore, the Jews were not considered to be the Lord's house. They were a chosen people, but God had another plan, a final plan, that was yet to be.

When the Lord's house was established, then the Word of the Lord would go forth from the place where it then was (Isaiah 2:3). The law would also go forth. From that place and time, "He will teach us of His ways, and we will walk in His paths." The establishment of the house of the Lord, then, preceded the spreading of the Word of the Lord.

THE PEOPLE

"All nations shall flow to it." The Lord's house, once established, would include people from all nations. This was a hard thing for Jews to hear. They were God's chosen people and they just could not imagine a time when even Gentiles would be numbered among them. Yet, Isaiah's prophecy said that very thing.

THE CITY

The identity of the city wherein this event would occur is very clear. The location is the top of a mountain (Isaiah 2:2-3). The place is called "Zion." That mountainous place, called Zion, is then named Jerusalem. Geographically, Jerusalem is situated among the hills surrounded by the valleys of Hinnom and Kidron. The Mount of Olives is also nearby. This is the mountainous region that Isaiah spoke of in his prophecy.

THE PROPHECY OF JESUS

Jesus also prophesied that He would build His Church (Matthew 16:13-20). Following Peter's confession that he believed Jesus to be "the Christ, the son of the living God" (v. 16). Jesus said in v. 18, "And I also say to you that you are Peter, and on this rock I will build My church, and the gates of Hades shall not prevail against it" (NKJV). Jesus used the occasion of Peter's confession to tell His disciples about the foundation upon which His Church would be built. The rock to which He referred was the "rock" of Peter's confession. The foundation of the Church that Jesus built was Peter's confession.

Furthermore, when He promised to build it, He said that "the gates of Hades shall not prevail against it." It is unfortunate that so many misunderstand what Jesus was saying here. "Hades" is called "hell" in the King James Version. However, Jesus is not speaking here about whether Satan would be able to stop what He was going to do.

The word "hades" means "the resting place of the dead." It is the place where all those who have died go to wait for the final judgment. Jesus was saying to His disciples that even His death would not stop the establishment of His Church. After Jesus died, He, too, went to the place where all the dead go (Acts 2:27).

ESTABLISHMENT OF THE CHURCH WAS FULFILLED AS PROPHESIED

Jesus' words to Peter following his confession are quite interesting. He said, "Blessed are you, Simon Bar-Jonah! For flesh and blood has not revealed this to you, but my Father who is in heaven. And I tell you, you are Peter, and on this rock I will build my church, and the gates of hell shall not prevail against it. I will give you the keys of the kingdom of heaven, and whatever you bind on earth shall be bound in heaven, and whatever you loose on earth shall be loosed in heaven" (Matthew 16:17-19).

After Jesus told Peter that He would build His Church, He promised to give to Peter the keys of the kingdom. Now, it does not make sense that Jesus would promise to build one thing and hand Peter the keys to something else. Jesus used the terms "kingdom of Heaven" and "Church" to refer to the same thing. This is corroborated in a series of New Testament texts wherein Jesus referred to the coming of the kingdom.

- "Truly, I say to you, there are some standing here who will not taste death until they see the Son of Man coming in his kingdom" (Matthew 16:28).
- "Truly, I say to you, there are some standing here who will not taste death until they see the kingdom of God after it has come with power" (Mark 9:1).

- "But I tell you truly, there are some standing here who will not taste death until they see the kingdom of God" (Luke 9:27).

These passages present two facts:

1. The kingdom of God was coming within the lifetimes of some of the people to whom Jesus was then speaking.

2. They would see the kingdom of God come with power.

The natural question is, what was the power that they saw signaling the coming of the kingdom of God? The answer to that question lies in two other New Testament passages. The first of these is Luke 24:46-49. This text records some of the last words that Jesus said to His disciples before He ascended back into Heaven. "Thus it is written, that the Christ should suffer and on the third day rise from the dead, and that repentance and forgiveness of sins should be proclaimed in his name to all nations, beginning from Jerusalem. You are witnesses of these things. And behold, I am sending the promise of my Father upon you. But stay in the city until you are clothed with power from on high."

In this statement, Jesus referred to "all nations" and to "Jerusalem" (remember the prophecy of Isaiah). He also told them of the power that was going to come upon them in Jerusalem. It was a power that was going to come upon them from God.

The second text is Acts 1:8. These words were also spoken by Jesus to His disciples immediately before His ascension. He said, "But you will receive power when the Holy Spirit has come upon you, and you will be my witnesses in Jerusalem and in all Judea and Samaria, and to the end of the earth."

There is an unmistakable connection between all of these verses. When they are all considered together, the message is clear. Jesus promised to build His Church and give Peter the keys of the kingdom. He also said that the coming of the kingdom would be signaled by a power that would be given to the disciples. Jesus used the terms "kingdom" and "Church" interchangeably, so what He promised about the one, He also meant for the other. Thus, on the same day that the disciples received the power, the kingdom or Church would come. The only thing left for us now is to determine when all of this occurred.

The passage that brings all of this together is Acts 2:1-4: "When the day of Pentecost arrived, they were all together in one place. And suddenly there came from heaven a sound like a mighty rushing wind, and it filled the entire house where they were sitting. And divided tongues as of fire appeared to them and rested on each one of them. And they were all filled with the Holy Spirit and began to speak in other tongues as the Spirit gave them utterance."

The time frame of this text is the "latter days." It is the time in which God has spoken through His Son. The disciples of Jesus are the ones on whom the Spirit came. Acts 2:14 confirms this. This event occurred in Jerusalem. It happened on a day when "all nations" were gathered (Acts 2:5).

Remember, also, Jesus promised that many who were listening to Him would see the kingdom of God coming with power, the power was promised to the apostles, and the power would come with the Spirit. On this occasion, the Spirit came to the apostles with the power to speak in languages that they had never studied. This power was evident to everyone (Acts 2:7). The subsequent sermon by Peter, in which he delivered "the keys of the kingdom" ushered the kingdom into existence. Three thousand people were obedient to the message that he preached (Acts 2:41).

With the convergence of all of these various things, there can be no doubt that this was the event Isaiah looked forward to and that

Jesus promised. On this day, the Church that Jesus promised began. On this day, the kingdom of Heaven came in the form of the Church that Jesus established.

We know for certain that by the time of the writing of Colossians 1:13, the kingdom had been established. "He has delivered us from the domain of darkness and transferred us to the kingdom of his beloved Son." The clear teaching of Scripture is that the Church/kingdom that God promised through prophets and through His Son was established on the first Pentecost after the resurrection of Jesus from the dead. Pentecost was, and is, a Jewish feast that occurs 50 days after Passover (Leviticus 23:15-16). It was a Sunday.

This Church is the kingdom of God into which all Christians, (Acts 11:26) have been translated. There are various terms in Scripture by which the Church is described. Any of these terms that we would use today to identify the gathering of Christians has the authority of the Bible. The term "Church of Christ" has continued because of its distinctiveness from the other terms. The other terms carry with them certain beliefs and practices that differ from what churches of Christ teach, but are observed in those churches that wear those particular names.

The Bride of Christ	Ephesians 5:22-32
The Body	Colossians 1:18
One Body	1 Corinthians 12:18-24
The Body of Christ	Ephesians 4:12
The Church	Ephesians 3:21
The Church of the Firstborn	Hebrews 12:23
The Church of God	1 Cornthians 1:2
The Church of the Living God	1 Timothy 3:15
The Churches of Christ	Romans 16:16
The City of God	Hebrews 12:22
The Flock	Acts 20:28

The Flock of God	1 Peter 5:2
Habitation of God	Ephesians 2:22
God's Building	1 Corinthians 3:9
God's Husbandry	1 Corinthians 3:9
Household of God	Ephesians 2:19
Israel of God	Galatians 6:16
Kingdom	Heberews 12:28
Kingdom of God's Dear Son	Colossians 1:13
People of God	1 Peter 2:10
Spiritual House	1 Peter 2:5
Temple of God	1 Corinthians 3:16
Mount Zion	Hebrews 12:22

REVIEW QUESTIONS

1. What term is synonymous with the kingdom of Heaven?

2. What does Jesus say about the kingdom of Heaven in Matthew 16:18 and Luke 9:27?

3. Who would give the apostles their power?

4. When did these things occur, or on what day was the Church established?

5. What miracle did the apostles experience in Acts 2:1-4?

6. What or who empowered them to do this?

7. What was so miraculous about this act?

8. Who preached the first sermon in the Church?

9. What was his message?

10. What did Paul write in Colossians 1:13 that applies to this study?

11. What did this prove about the Church?

12. What day of the week was the day of Pentecost on?

13. List some of the names for the Church found in the Scriptures.

14. What is the book, chapter, and verse where the term "churches of Christ" is used?

15. How is the Church described in Ephesians 5:22-32?

16. How is the Church described in Ephesians 4:12?

17. From what year can we date the Roman Catholic church?

18. Of what significance is this?

4

ORGANIZATION OF THE CHURCH

When we talk about the organization of the Church, we refer to the government of the Church. We do not find the organization of the Church, including any rule or authority, outside of the local setting. That is, the churches of Christ are autonomous. They govern and rule themselves under a specific organization that is found in the Scriptures.

Autonomous means "self-ruled." It means that there is no organization or order that is higher than or greater than the local Church. No conventions are held to make laws or take votes on anything that is done in the various congregations of the churches of Christ. This is the way the Bible presents the organization of the early Church, and we believe this is the way that it is to be done today.

In our study, we will consider five main passages of Scripture: Acts 20:28; 1 Timothy 3:1-13; Titus 1:5-9; Hebrews 13:17; and 1 Peter 5:1-4. We will also consider the various words that are used to describe those who fill the role of elder within the Church.

ELDERS

The ideal organization for each local congregation is to have elders who rule there. Paul wrote to Titus that he was to "put what remained into order" (Titus 1:5). He fulfilled his mission as he appointed elders in every city.

WHERE DO THEY OPERATE?

Each time we see elders from a specific locale mentioned in Scripture, they always appear in the plural. As in Titus 1:5, the text shows us that there should be a plurality of elders in a given congregation. It is not proper for a single person to rule.

These elders function within the local Church only. In 1 Peter 5:1-4, we find Peter's admonition to the elders who served in various places in the known world (1 Peter 1:1). He told them where they were to exercise this service and authority. He said, "Shepherd the flock of God that is among you" (1 Peter 5:2). They were to lead and guide the Church among them, that is, where they lived and served. Nowhere is there any authority for elders to operate outside the local setting or Church.

WHAT IS THEIR FUNCTION?

Hebrews 13:17 tells us what the function of elders is and what the function of the people under them is: "Obey your leaders and submit to them, for they are keeping watch over your souls, as those who will have to give an account. Let them do this with joy and not with groaning, for that would be of no advantage to you."

Here we find that elders have authority over the congregation in which they operate. This authority is the rule for the members of the Church. However, they are not to be "domineering over those in your charge" (1 Peter 5:3). Those within the Church are to obey them and be submissive to them.

Elders function in God's plan for the governance of the Church. Their authority does not give them the right to change anything that God has already decided. Their rule extends to carrying out that which God has told the Church to do. Elders rule in matters of judgment and methodology. They are the ones appointed to decide how to carry out God's instructions for the local Church.

No good eldership, however, would dare set itself up in an ivory tower and simply hand down commands for the Church. Proper judgment would indicate that they obtain input from the congregation in their decision-making process. This input is not in the form of democratic rule, but it is valuable for the elders to consider in deciding the best course for the Church.

QUALIFICATIONS FOR ELDERS

Titus 1:5-9 and 1 Timothy 3:1-7 give us the qualifications of those who would be elders in the local Church. The following chart compares the two passages.

1 TIMOTHY 3:1-7	TITUS 1:5-9
the husband of one wife v. 2	the husband of one wife v. 6
temperate v. 2	not quick-tempered v. 7
sober-minded v. 2	sober-minded v. 8
of good behavior v. 2	holy v. 8
hospitable v. 2	hospitable v. 8
able to teach v. 2	holding fast to the word v. 9
not given to wine v. 3	not given to wine v. 7

1 TIMOTHY 3:1-7	TITUS 1:5-9
not violent v. 3	not violent v. 7
not greedy for money v. 3	not greedy for money v. 7
gentle v. 3	self-controlled v. 8
not quarrelsome v. 3	not self-willed v. 7
not covetous v. 3	lover of what is good v. 8
rules his own house well vv. 4-5	having faithful children v. 6
not a novice v. 6	just v. 8
of good report from without v. 7	

TERMS FOR ELDERS

There are three basic words used to describe these men. The terms are *elder*, *bishop*, and *pastor*. Each of these words highlights a special part of the function of those who govern the local Church in this way. "Elder" signifies the age of the man who serves. He is older and, therefore, able to rule based on his maturity and experience.

"Bishop" describes the function of overseeing that is given to the men who are the rulers and governors of the Church. In this function, they are the guardians or superintendents of the entire operation of the local congregation.

"Pastor" and "shepherd" are the same terms. As shepherds, these men are concerned for the spiritual well-being of the sheep (or members) of the local congregation. As the physical shepherd provides sustenance to his sheep, these spiritual shepherds provide for the spiritual sustenance of their sheep. In this role, they are concerned for what is taught and done within the confines of their sphere of operation.

DEACONS

These men are the leaders whose primary concern is the day-to-day operation of the physical affairs of the congregation. However, their tasks are necessary for the spiritual operation of the congregation, as well, for they handle the nuts and bolts of putting into motion the activities of the congregation.

The word *deacon* simply means "servant" or "one who serves." In this capacity, deacons put their special talents to work in behalf of various projects and on-going areas of work to oversee that the work is carried out. Their authority is a delegated authority given to them by the elders of the local congregation to carry out the specific tasks that are given to them.

Those who would be deacons must also meet certain requirements. These characteristics are enumerated in 1 Timothy 3:8-13.

PREACHER & TEACHERS

The preacher is hired to preach, teach, study, and aid in the growth and development of the congregation. His primary function is to inform others of the Word of God. His function does not include enforcement of those things. Elders take the lead in the enforcement of the various aspects of the Christian life that the Bible determines are necessary for everyone.

Teachers are given the responsibility to transmit the information within the Word of God that is deemed necessary to be taught at a particular time to the various age groups within the congregation. They, of necessity, are members who manifest spirituality and biblical understanding relative to the group that they are to teach. The elders are ultimately responsible for the content of the various classes. Certain deacons have the responsibility for determining the specific classes that teachers will be teaching at a given time.

REVIEW QUESTIONS

1. What does the word "autonomous" mean?

2. Why does the Church not have an organizational structure outside the local congregational level?

3. Why did Paul leave Titus in Crete according to Titus 1:5?

4. What should be the attitude of the people over whom the elders rule?

5. We know that elders have authority, but what do they not have authority to do?

6. What other terms describe the same office?

7. What is the definition of "deacon"?

5

MISSION OF THE CHURCH

"And he gave the apostles, the prophets, the evangelists, the shepherds and teachers, to equip the saints for the work of ministry, for building up the body of Christ" (Ephesians 4:11-12). God's mission for the Church is three-fold. It includes:

- Education — "equipping the saints"
- Evangelism — "work of the ministry"
- Edification — "the edifying of the body of Christ"

This mission is the standard by which each congregation of the Church should examine itself. The goal of the Church should be the same goal of her head, Jesus. He said of the goal of His life, "I must be about My Father's business" (Luke 2:49 NKJV).

EDUCATION : "EQUIPPING THE SAINTS"

Education matures Christians. First Peter 2:1-2 teaches that each Christian is under an obligation before God to grow. "Therefore, laying aside all malice, all deceit, hypocrisy, envy, and all evil speaking, as newborn babes, desire the pure milk of the word, that you may grow thereby."

The milk of the word is used at the beginning of the growth process. No newborn baby can be fed a diet of steak. Likewise, no newborn Christian is ready for the meat of the word. "But I, brothers, could not address you as spiritual people, but as people of the flesh, as infants in Christ. I fed you with milk, not solid food, for you were not ready for it. And even now you are not yet ready" (1 Corinthians 3:1-2).

Growth occurs as we add to our lives the things that bring us to maturity before God. Second Peter 1:5-7 records, "For this very reason, make every effort to supplement your faith with virtue, and virtue with knowledge, and knowledge with self-control, and self-control with steadfastness, and steadfastness with godliness, and godliness with brotherly affection, and brotherly affection with love" (Hebrews 5:12-14).

Education supports homes. The primary responsibility for the training of children lies with parents in the home (Ephesians 6:1-4). The Church should, though, support their training through its education process. What is taught from the pulpit and from the individual classrooms must support the spiritual training that is taking place within each home. Where parents are doing their job to train their children for the Lord, the Church takes a supportive role. Where parents are failing, the Church must take a primary role.

Education aids the shepherds as they watch over the souls of the members. Shepherds feed the flock (Acts 20:28). A shepherd of sheep makes certain that there is plenty of water and food. Spiritual shepherds provide for the spiritual food and drink of each member. Through classes and preaching, education supports the leadership of the local shepherds.

Shepherds oversee the flock. They should know what is going on with the members of the church where they serve. Therefore, they should know and control what is being taught in every phase of education whether from the pulpit or in the classroom (Acts 20:2).

Shepherds lead the flock. They are in front of the sheep leading them in the way that they want them to go. They do not stand at the rear and order the sheep into the pasture. Neither do they walk behind them and drive them into the pasture. This is one of the reasons that God required elders to be "able to teach" (1 Timothy 3:2). They should be involved in the teaching of the educational work of the local church.

EVANGELISM: "WORK OF THE MINISTRY"

Evangelism is the life-blood of the Lord's Church. Unless we reach out to others, the Church will cease to exist. Every work of the Church should play some part in the mission of evangelizing a lost and dying world. The evangelistic message today must be the same message preached in the churches of the first century. Paul wrote in 1 Corinthians 2:2, "For I decided to know nothing among you except Jesus Christ and him crucified." This is the gospel message (1 Corinthians 15:1-4; 2 Thessalonians 1:6-9).

The evangelistic plan today must be the same plan used in the churches of the first century. What they did and did not do teaches us about our evangelistic plans. Their plan did not include some things that have, unfortunately, been done in churches of today.

1. They did not wait around for the lost to visit them when they were assembled for worship. The time of worship was not for the lost primarily. It was for the saved to praise the God of Heaven. Acts 8:26-40 is an example of a Christian going out to find someone who needed to hear. He took the message to

the person.

2. They did not put all the responsibility for spreading the gospel message on a hired preacher. Sure, there were preachers who did this full time (Paul is a good example). But, everyone taught as they had opportunity (Acts 8:4).

3. They did not wait for an organized "evangelism program" to be started in order to be evangelistic. Can you imagine Paul or Peter standing up in a worship assembly of the first century and inviting anyone to the front who wanted to be involved in evangelism?

4. The first-century church did not get their converts primarily from public preaching. When Saul persecuted the Church (Acts 8:33), he did so by entering into the members' houses. It is reasonable to assume that this is where he found them spreading the message of Jesus.

5. The first-century Church did not give the people what they wanted to hear. They preached what they needed to hear. A fundamental change in this very point was predicted in 2 Timothy 4:1-4. God said that there was coming a time when people would "not endure sound doctrine." Rather, they would "heap up for themselves teachers" who would tickle their "itching ears" and not teach sound doctrine.

6. They, also, avoided preaching and teaching a message fashioned after their own desires. They presented the message just as God delivered it to them. They took their authority from words such as these from Paul to Timothy, "Preach the word; be ready in season and out of season; reprove, rebuke, and exhort, with complete patience and teaching" (2 Timothy 4:2).

The evangelistic plan of the first-century Church included at least three important things. They prayed for evangelistic fervor

(Acts 4:23-30). They were supportive of sound preaching (Galatians 2:9). And they practiced the great commission (Matthew 28:18-20) to such a degree that they spread the gospel to the known world during that first century (Colossians 1:23).

The evangelistic goal today must be the same goal advanced in the churches of the first century. Their goal was to disturb the peace of people and offer them real peace from Jesus (Acts 17:1-9). We can track this disruption of peace in the book of Acts:

- When people heard about the resurrection of Jesus, they were "greatly disturbed" (4:2).
- When they heard a message about sin, some were indignant (5:17, 28).
- The preaching about the cessation of the Old Law caused people to be "stirred up" (6:12-14).
- There was "no small dissension" (15:1-2).
- And, the teachers were "opposed" (18:6, 13).
- When Jesus was identified as the Christ, the people "plotted to kill" (9:22-23) the teacher.
- The acceptance of the Gentiles into the fellowship caused "contention" (11:2-3).
- Paul's preaching about the only true God moved the people to stone him at Lystra (14:19).
- And, when he preached that message in Ephesus, a commotion erupted (19:23).
- The people responded to the message of Paul's conversion and "raised their voices, tore their clothes, and threw dust into the air" (22:22-23).

The conversion process today is no different. We still must disturb the peace. We must disturb the peace they have in trusting in themselves and turn them to trust in Jesus (Acts 16:31). We must disturb the peace they have in following their own path and turn them to the only path that leads to eternal life through their repentance (Acts 3:19).

We must disturb the peace of self-allegiance and replace it with an allegiance to Jesus Christ through their confession of Him as Lord and Savior (1 Timothy 6:12-13). We must disturb the peace that people have from believing that they are in a safe condition and replace it with a real, restored innocence through baptism for the remission of sins (Acts 2:38). This is how we disturb the peace of people today and replace it with the peace of Jesus.

EDIFICATION: "THE EDIFYING OF THE BODY OF CHRIST"

Paul wrote that we are to be "eager to maintain the unity of the Spirit in the bond of peace" (Ephesians 4:3). Fellowship is the key to this. Without fellowship, there is nothing on which to build a bond that will bind us together. The first-century Church experienced great things because of their continuing and fervent fellowship (Acts 2:40-47). Their fellowship developed:

- community-wide respect for the Church (v. 43)
- a congregational oneness (v. 44)
- an awareness of the needs of the people within the Church (v. 45)
- congregational joy and humility (v. 46)
- community-wide favor for the Church (v. 47)
- Church growth (v. 48)

Fervent and continual fellowship within the Church today will yield the same results. That is why God wants us to "exhort one another daily" (Hebrews 3:13). There is also a fellowship element to the weekly assembly that God instructs us to have (Hebrews 10:24-25).

If the same message is preached today, it will yield the same results. Christians will be added to the Lord's Church wherein they will work to support the mission that God has given the Church to fulfill. That mission is to evangelize the lost, educate the saved, and edify the body.

REVIEW QUESTIONS

1. What is the three-fold mission of the Church?

2. What does education do?

3. What is the goal of education in the Church?

4. What is the life-blood of the Church?

5. What did the first-century Church not do in evangelism?

6. What was the evangelistic goal of the Church of the first-century?

7. What is edification?

8. How does this benefit the Church?

6

WORSHIP:
DEFINITION

Many churches are caught in the crosshairs of an ongoing discussion. It is a discussion about the focus and structure of corporate or congregational worship. "What is worship?" lies at the core of this discussion. The proper way to answer this question is to find the biblical answer.

There are at least five primary words translated "worship" by one or two versions. The main word for worship is *proskuneo*. This word means, "to kiss the hand to (toward); to fall upon the knees and touch the ground with the forehead." This word is always translated, "worshipped, kneeled, or bowed." This is the word used in the text we will study. This is the definition of worship for the study: Worship is a planned time in which we honor God from the heart through actions proscribed by Him and because He demands it.

The text for this study is John 4:19-24. Jesus had a discussion with a Samaritan woman at Jacob's well. She came to realize that the one to whom she was speaking was special. She declared, "Sir, I perceive that you are a prophet" (v. 19). Her next words to Him concerned a major sticking point between the Jews and the Samaritans. It was a disagreement over worship. "Our fathers worshiped on this mountain, but you say that in Jerusalem is the place where people ought to worship" (v. 20). In Jesus' response, we find God's definition of worship.

WORSHIP IS MOMENTARY

The woman asked about worship in a certain place. The entire discussion is about worship. But, they were not worshipping at that particular time. This is a significant point because there are many who operate under the premise that all of life is worship. That is, they believe that everything a Christian does in life is worship to God.

This misunderstanding comes from an improper rendering of Romans 12:1 in the New International Version. This version translates the verse, "Therefore, I urge you, brothers and sisters, in view of God's mercy, to offer your bodies as a living sacrifice, holy and pleasing to God—this is your true and proper worship." This is translated from the Greek word *latreuo*. Of the major versions, only one other, the New American Standard Version, also translates this word as "worship." But the primary meaning of the word is "service." Since the vast majority of the versions use the word "service" instead of "worship," it is proper to prefer "service" over "worship" in this text. This is the proper way to approach Bible study in different versions.

A common sense approach to the text validates this point. Jesus and the Samaritan woman were not worshipping at the time they were discussing worship. Jesus certainly was in the service of God by having the discussion. But, neither He nor she were worshipping while they were talking.

This same thing is true in other texts. The Ethiopian Eunuch "had come to Jerusalem to worship" (Acts 8:27). He was not worshipping on the way to or from Jerusalem. Paul mentioned a time when he "went up to Jerusalem to worship" (Acts 24:11). Paul was not worshipping on his way to Jerusalem. There are many other texts that teach the same principle, but these are sufficient to show that worship is momentary; it has a beginning and an end.

So, how do we refer to the rest of the Christian life? The Bible does not call it worship. The Bible calls it a walk: "walk in the Spirit" (Galatians 5:16); "walk in the light" (1 John 1:7); "walk as children of light" (Ephesians 5:8); "walk in love" (Ephesians 5:2).

WORSHIP IS INTENTIONAL

Jesus told the woman that true worshippers "will worship" (v. 23). He presented the concept of worship as a fact to be observed. He used the word "will" to describe that fact. Worship, then, is something that we decide to do. It is not accidental. It is not even possible to worship accidentally.

How strange would it sound to blurt out in the midst of a group of people, "Hey, I just worshipped, and I didn't even realize it!" If worship cannot be accidental, it must be intentional. It must be something that we decide to do at a particular time. Worship engages the body and the mind.

WORSHIP IS PERSONAL

Jesus referred to "worshippers" in v. 23. He has in mind each person who chooses to worship at a particular time. Worship cannot be done vicariously. That is, we cannot allow someone to worship for us. Worship is participatory and not observatory.

There is no thought in the mind of Jesus that we may consider ourselves to have worshipped just because we are in the presence of people who are, themselves, engaged in worship. Worship is personal. It must be done by the individual. We cannot refrain from worship and then claim to have worshipped just because we sat in the presence of those who did worship.

WORSHIP IS VERTICAL

Jesus identified for the woman the object of all worship—"the Father" (v. 23). Worship that is directed to the Father requires that two things happen. First, God must be in focus. We worship God only when we direct our attention to God as we worship. God is in focus when He is the center of our worship. God is in focus when He is the foundation of our worship.

Second, self must be out of focus. God did not design worship primarily for me. He designed worship primarily for the One who should be in focus during our worship—God our Father. Since worship was not designed primarily for me, my feelings after a time of worship are not the standard of measurement of the success of the worship experience.

Those who say, following a time of corporate worship, "I just did not get anything out of that service," say more about themselves than about the service itself. If I get nothing out of a particular time of worship, it is obvious that I did not put anything into it. My feelings following a time of worship are a by-product not a goal. Worship was not designed primarily to stimulate my feelings. However, when I worship as I should, I will be changed positively.

WORSHIP IS INTERNAL

Worship begins internally in the heart and moves externally into evident actions. Jesus told the woman, "God is spirit, and those who worship him must worship in spirit..." (v. 24). God is a spiritual being. The spirit is the essence of a being. It is the spirit of a man who "knows the things of a man" (1 Corinthians 2:11). It is our spirit or the essence of our hearts that generates our worship to God.

External effects cannot produce worship that is not already resident in the heart. External effects (lighting, power point, etc.) might enhance or diminish worship, but they do not create worship. Preparation for worship should include preparing our hearts to worship.

WORSHIP IS STRUCTURED

Jesus spoke to this woman about true worship in v. 23. Since He spoke of true worship, it is evident that there is such a thing as false or untrue worship. Worship can be done wrong. But, worship can and should be done right. Furthermore, it is evident that we can know the difference.

Jesus spoke of "true worshipers" who will worship the Father. True worshipers, then, are guided to worship the Father as directed by Him. It is not possible for us to know of our own accord how to worship God. The acceptable actions of worship must be determined by God.

WORSHIP IS RESPONSIVE

Jesus continued with these words in v. 23, "the Father is seeking such people to worship him." Worship is the response we give to the Father's seeking. He wants and desires our worship. Furthermore, He deserves our worship since He is God.

Worship is the response we give to the Father's guidance. He is interested in true worship. We should seek His guidance in order to worship as He desires. Seeking His guidance is the proper response.

Why? Man has never been free to design his own worship of God. Nadab and Abihu (Leviticus 10) and Jeroboam (1 Kings 12:25-33) teach this very clearly.

WORSHIP IS NECESSARY

Finally, Jesus said to the woman at the well, "God is spirit, and those who worship him must worship in spirit and truth" (v. 24). Jesus is not saying, "If you choose to worship God, worship Him in spirit and truth." He is not giving anyone the option to choose not to worship Him and still be pleasing to Him. Instead, He says, "Those who choose to worship God (and that is the only choice I can make if I desire to be His faithful child), must worship Him in spirit and truth." Worshipping God is necessary for each person. No one has the right to choose not to worship and still expect God's grace and mercy.

Understanding God's definition of worship is necessary in order to be pleasing to Him. If we let God speak to us on this matter through His word, we can be certain that He will be pleased with our worship. Remember: Worship is a planned time in which we honor God from the heart through actions proscribed by Him and because He demands it.

REVIEW QUESTIONS

1. Who is the center of our worship?

2. What does it mean for God to be the center of our worship?

3. How might our worship be improper?

4. What are the proper attitudes to have in worship?

5. What are some things to consider as we prepare for worship?

6. Worship has a _____ and an _____.

7. We should always look for God's _____ when deciding what to do in worship.

7

WORSHIP: SINGING

The Bible authorizes singing that is free of any mechanically produced sounds, free of any vocally produced sounds, free of any solos, choirs, etc., and comprised of words that are sung by the group that "teach and admonish" those who are gathered for worship. This study seeks to define proper worship through song.

THE BIBLE AUTHORIZES

We are dealing in this study with what the Bible teaches—what it authorizes. We want to be what the Bible teaches the Church to be. Our model for that Church is the Church of the first century. The summation of their activity is found in Acts 2:42—"And they devoted themselves to the apostles' teaching and the fellowship, to the breaking of bread and the prayers."

In order to determine what the apostles' doctrine is, we need to study what they said and what the early Church did. By combining these things, we see an accurate picture of what God intends for the Church by His teaching in Scripture.

WORSHIP

This study is limited to our singing when approaching God in worship. It is not to be pulled into a discussion of other times when worship is not being engaged. This is not about listening to religious music on the radio or in person. Therefore, it is necessary for us to understand what worship is.

Look up the following verses and see that worship is defined in Scripture as an activity involving intention and that has a beginning and an end. In other words, worship is an intentional activity in which one decides to pay tribute to God in specific, predetermined ways (John 4:24). When, therefore, one has completed this, he returns to his normal life. This is not worship but is simply "walking in the Spirit" (Galatians 5:16). All of the following verses show that worship is something that is done in addition to or as a part of daily life.

- Matthew 2:2, 8, 11; 4:9; 8:2; 9:18; 14:33; 15:25; 18:26; 28:9
- Mark 5:6; 15:19
- Luke 4:7
- John 4:20; 9:38; 12:20
- Acts 8:27; 10:25; 24:11
- Revelation 3:9; 4:10; 15:4; 19:10; 22:8, 9

FREE OF ANY MECHANICALLY PRODUCED SOUNDS

This is how worship in song should be because that is what is taught specifically. Ephesians 5:18 teaches us to "be filled with the Spirit." There are five prepositional phrases that follow this command and all of them together complete the command to sing.

1. "addressing one another"
2. "singing"

3. "making melody"

4. "giving thanks...to God the Father"

5. "submitting to one another"

Colossians 3:16 teaches us to "let the word of Christ dwell in you richly." We are taught to do this by "teaching and admonishing one another in all wisdom, singing psalms and hymns and spiritual songs, with thankfulness in your hearts to God."

It is obvious that there are two types of music that we might use to praise God: vocal and mechanical. Both types of music were used in the Old Testament. It is our job to understand whether God wants both of these, one of these, or neither of these in worship to Him under the New Testament era.

He certainly expects one of these to be used because singing means one of them. The question is whether singing is exclusive of mechanical music. From this verse, it is easy to see that singing is exclusive of mechanical music because of how singing is defined.

According to this verse, singing teaches and admonishes. The only way to do this is with words. A mechanical instrument does not teach or admonish in any way. Therefore, since our singing is to teach and admonish, then the word "singing" only has reference to vocally produced words.

FREE OF ANY VOCALLY PRODUCED SOUNDS

By "vocally produced sounds," I mean making the sounds of instruments without actually playing the instruments. Again, what do the Scriptures teach? They teach that we are to "teach and admonish" with our singing.

These vocally produced sounds do not teach and admonish at all. They are an addition to what the Scriptures teach in the same way that the actual instruments are. We have no more authority to have the entire Church hum or whistle a particular song than we do to play it.

FREE OF ANY SOLOS, CHOIRS, ETC.

If the passages under consideration, Ephesians 5:19 and Colossians 3:16, are instructive to each Christian, then each Christian should be guided by them. In this case, the only authority we have is for each Christian to sing. There is no authority for listening to the singing.

The entire congregation is one choir before God. No one person or group of persons should entertain or display his or her talents above the others. When part of the group (for instance, the women) are singing while the other part of the group (for instance, the men) are silent during a song, they are functioning as a choir before the Lord composed of every member of Christ's gathered family.

There is a final point that needs to be made about the proper understanding of these passages. If singing includes mechanical instruments, how do we obey the teaching if only one person or a few persons are doing the playing? In other words, if the passages are instructing every faithful Christian how to approach God in worship through song, then wouldn't it mean that every Christian should play a mechanical instrument? If this verse teaches all Christians to sing (which includes mechanical music), why does it not also teach all Christians to play? This question must be answered by anyone who believes that the Scriptures that teach singing also authorize mechanical music.

REVIEW QUESTIONS

1. What does the phrase "the Bible authorizes" mean?

2. Why should we study what the Church in the first century did as a guide for us today?

3. What is worship?

4. How does "walking in the Spirit" (Galatians 5:16) differ from worship?

5. What two passages teach or authorize only singing to the Lord in worship?

6. How is "singing" defined in the two passages above?

7. Why should all Christians sing in worship to God?

8

WORSHIP: LORD'S SUPPER

When God's people in the early church came together for worship, they partook of the Lord's Supper. It was a time when they celebrated together the sacrifice of Jesus in behalf of his people. The Supper serves as a fitting reminder, not only of Jesus' death, but also of the unity that ought to characterize the body of Christ. We are all in the family together because of what Jesus did for us. We honor Him through this action.

WHO SHOULD TAKE THE SUPPER?

The Supper is for the Church. The Supper is for the family of God to commune together and celebrate that which unites all of us into one body—the death, burial, and resurrection of Jesus. Luke 22:14-20 records the night when Jesus instituted the Supper. Verses 19-20 read, "And he took bread, and when he had given thanks, he broke it and gave it to them, saying, 'This is my body, which is given for you. Do this in remembrance of me.' And likewise the cup after they had eaten, saying, 'This cup that is poured out for you is the new covenant in my blood.'"

Jesus clearly identified a special group of people—those for whom His body was broken and His blood was shed. These people not only have a special relationship with Him, but they also have a reason for participating in this Supper. The proper question to ask is, "For whom did Jesus give His body and shed His blood?" Once these people are known, it will be obvious who should take the supper.

Jesus gave His body and shed His blood in His death on the cross. Paul writes concerning these people, "we have now been justified by his blood" (Romans 5:9). The cross was God's chosen method to bring salvation to the entire world. Those who accept the sacrifice of Jesus are the people who should take the Supper as a memorial of the death of Jesus and what that death has provided them.

WHAT SHOULD WE USE?

In 1 Corinthians 11, Paul recalled the night that Jesus instituted this Supper. He said, "For I received from the Lord what I also delivered to you, that the Lord Jesus on the night when he was betrayed took bread... In the same way also he took the cup, after supper" (vv. 23, 25). Paul delivered to the Corinthians the same practice that Jesus set up the night before His death. And God intended for all Christians to observe this supper, for Paul continued in v. 26, "For as often as you eat this bread and drink the cup, you proclaim the Lord's death until he comes."

"And as they were eating, he took bread... And he took a cup..." (Mark 14:22-23). Two verses later, we learn that the cup was "fruit of the vine" (v. 25). The Lord's Supper was instituted during Jesus' observance of the Passover with His disciples (Mark 14:12). This feast was held yearly in remembrance of the time when God passed over the children of Israel and did not kill all their firstborn as He did the firstborn of the Egyptians under whom they had been enslaved (Exodus 12).

The Passover meal included a lamb, unleavened bread, and bitter herbs (Exodus 12:3, 8). It is obvious from the context of Mark 14:25, that "fruit of the vine" was also a part of the meal. Jesus took the fruit of the vine and the unleavened bread and attached a new meaning to them. He had each of the apostles take of them with this new meaning in mind (Mark 14:22-23).

Of the unleavened bread, Jesus said, "Take; this is my body" (Mark 14:22) Of the fruit of the vine, He said, "This is my blood of the covenant, which is poured out for many" (Mark 14:24) Unleavened bread and fruit of the vine are still the emblems that God expects us to use in our observance of the Lord's Supper today. We have no authority to substitute or to add anything else to the Supper.

WHEN SHOULD THE SUPPER BE OBSERVED?

The record of Scripture reveals, "On the first day of the week, when we were gathered together to break bread" (Acts 20:7). How did they know to do what they did? Where did they receive their authority for their actions?

Acts 2:42 provides the answer to these questions. "And they devoted themselves to the apostles' teaching and the fellowship, to the breaking of bread and the prayers." Everything the disciples did in the worship of the church was based on the authority they received from the apostles' doctrine.

The weekly assembly of Christians on the first day of the week was the response of the Christians to the teaching of the apostles. This is also the same day that the Church Jesus promised to build (Matthew 16:18-19) came into existence. That day was the "Day of Pentecost" (Acts 2:1).

The Day of Pentecost is defined in Leviticus 23:16, "You shall count fifty days to the day after the seventh Sabbath." The Jews also called this feast the Feast of Weeks (Exodus 34:22). When you count fifty days after the seventh Sabbath following Passover, you come to the first day of the week or Sunday.

Thus, the authority of Scripture is that the disciples gathered on the first day of the week to partake of the Lord's Supper. Since there is a first day of the week every week, their practice is our authority for observing that practice today. We have no authority to substitute a different day or to add another day.

WHY SHOULD WE TAKE THIS SUPPER?

Jesus left His disciples some final instructions before He ascended back to His Father. Matthew 28:20 records, "teaching them to observe all that I have commanded you." The reason that they assembled on the first day of the week was because they had been taught to do that by the apostles (Acts 2:42). They were even instructed not to forsake assembling together (Hebrews 10:25).

The purpose of the Supper lies in the concept of unity. Paul wrote to the Corinthian Church about the Lord's Supper in 1 Corinthians 11:17-34. He addressed a problem in the Church concerning the abuse of the Supper.

There were "divisions" (v. 18) and "factions" (v. 19) among them. These divisions and factions arose out of a situation described in v. 21, "...each one goes ahead with his own meal. One goes hungry, another gets drunk." When they came together, it appears that they were segregating themselves from each other and taking of the Supper in separate groups.

The main separation was between the rich and the poor. Paul said in v. 22, "Do you despise the church of God and humiliate those who have nothing?" The Supper should be a time when there is unity and not division. The Supper is for those who "come together as a church" (v. 18). For this reason, Paul closed his message to this church with a clear admonition. "So then, my brothers, when you come together to eat, wait for one another" (v. 33).

HOW SHOULD WE OBSERVE THIS SUPPER?

Again, 1 Corinthians 11:17-34 provides the answer to this question. Particularly, vv. 26-27 record, "For as often as you eat this bread and drink the cup, you proclaim the Lord's death until he comes. Whoever, therefore, eats the bread or drinks the cup of the Lord in an unworthy manner will be guilty concerning the body and blood of the Lord."

We must observe the Supper in a worthy manner. This is not to say that we are to determine if we are worthy to take the Supper. Only through Jesus can I be worthy anyway. I am not worthy on my own. It is the manner in which we take the Supper that is of concern here. Notice how Paul defines the worthy manner in partaking the Supper. The Supper was given to help us remember. We are to remember Jesus and His life, death, and resurrection.

"For I received from the Lord what I also delivered to you, that the Lord Jesus on the night when he was betrayed took bread, and when he had given thanks, he broke it, and said, 'This is my body which is for you. Do this in remembrance of me.' In the same way also he took the cup, after supper, saying, 'This cup is the new covenant in my blood. Do this, as often as you drink it, in remembrance of me.'" (vv. 23-25)

The Supper was given to us to take until Jesus returns again. "For as often as you eat this bread and drink the cup, you proclaim the Lord's death until he comes" (v. 26). The Supper was given to cause us to examine ourselves. Partaking of the Supper is a good time for reflection on our lives and for determining that we are going to do a better job of living for the One who died for us. "Let a person examine himself, then, and so eat of the bread and drink of the cup" (v. 28).

Finally, as we take the Supper, we should reflect on our place within the body of Christ. We need to consider whether we are aiding the body of Christ with our lives or whether we are hindering the body of Christ with our lives. "For anyone who eats and drinks without discerning the body eats and drinks judgment on himself" (v. 29).

The Lord's Supper is a vital part of our worship of God. He wants His people, Christians, to gather together on the first day of the week to remember the death of Jesus on the cross. If we want to be like those first Christians who practiced what the apostles taught them (Acts 2:42), we will take the Lord's Supper seriously.

REVIEW QUESTIONS

1. What is the purpose of the Lord's Supper?

2. For whom is the Lord's Supper intended?

3. Why should we use unleavened bread and fruit of the vine in the Lord's Supper?

4. The Lord's Supper is based on what Jewish feast?

5. What foods were used in that feast?

6. Why do we partake of the Lord's Supper on the first day of the week?

7. The Lord's Church started on what Jewish feast day?

8. How does the Lord's Supper bring unity to the group?

9. How are we worthy to partake of the Lord's Supper?

10. How do we take the Lord's Supper in a worthy manner?

9

WORSHIP: GIVING

Jesus uttered a powerful truth in Matthew 6:21, "For where your treasure is, there your heart will be also." A famous radio talk show host uses the phrase, "Follow the money" when looking for the motive behind some action. Both of these statements refer to the same concept. We are influenced and, sometimes, controlled by money.

The way we use our money is probably a good barometer of our priorities. Those things we prize highly get the lion's-share. A Christian needs to consider well how much money he will give to the Lord for the on-going work of the church. Free-will giving is an indication of one's commitment level as a Christian.

THE FIRST CHRISTIANS WERE GIVERS

The first Christians demonstrated their giving attitude immediately after obeying the gospel. Acts 2:44-45 records, "And all who believed were together and had all things in common. And they were selling their possessions and belongings and distributing the proceeds to all, as any had need."

They were motivated to act this way because no one thought "that any of the things that belonged to him was his own, but they had everything in common" (Acts 4:32). Therefore, "there was not a needy person among them, for as many as were owners of lands or houses sold them and brought the proceeds of what was sold and laid it at the apostles' feet, and it was distributed to each as any had need (4:34-35).

When a great famine arose in the land of Judea, Christians from all over the world sent relief to them. Those first Christians were giving people. It is this famine and the subsequent giving of Christians to relieve those in need that provides a good insight into proper giving.

WHAT IS PROPER GIVING?

The entire context of 2 Corinthians 8:1-9:15 deals with this famine and those who sent aid. The text provides the characteristics of proper giving. Proper giving originates with a willingness to give myself to God first (2 Corinthians 8:1-7).

Paul held up the churches of Macedonia as examples of this. Not only were they willing to give (v. 2), but they were willing to give even though they were in great affliction (v. 2). Paul said that they gave "beyond their ability" (v. 3). In v. 5, Paul revealed why they were able to do this: "They gave themselves first to the Lord and then by the will of God to us."

Proper giving grows out of love for God and for others (2 Corinthians 8:8-15). Paul used the example of the Macedonian Christians to inspire and challenge the Christians in Corinth to be givers. He said, "I say this not as a command, but to prove by the earnestness of others that your love also is genuine" (v. 8).

Jesus is the supreme example of love-motivated-giving. "For you know the grace of our Lord Jesus Christ, that though he was rich, yet for your sake he became poor, so that you by his poverty might become rich" (v. 9). Paul urged the Corinthians to follow through with their commitment and give to the Judean famine as they had determined (vv. 10-11). It was their love for people suffering through the famine that should drive them to give.

The goal of their giving was that there would be equality among all (vv. 12-15). There was not complete equality of financial resources, but there was complete equality among all who gave in that they all participated together. By giving, they closed the gap between themselves and those who received their gift.

Proper giving is a reflection of the love that I have (2 Corinthians 8:16-24). In v. 24, Paul urged the Corinthians to "give proof before the churches of your love and of our boasting about you." These people had a love for those in need and Paul had already told others about their love. Through their giving, they confirmed what Paul had said.

Proper giving demands preparation (2 Corinthians 9:1-5). These Christians in Corinth were willing to give. They had already decided a year before that they would be involved in the effort (vv. 1-2). Now, it was time to do what they had committed to do. Paul sent some people ahead to make sure that the Corinthians were prepared to give so that they would not be ashamed when the time came to give the money (vv. 3-4). Preparation to give keeps you from being ashamed at the time of giving. Paul told them to "arrange in advance for the gift you have promised, so that it may be ready as a willing gift, not as an exaction" (v. 5).

Proper giving follows the giving principle (2 Corinthians 9:6-9). There are three parts to this giving principle. The first part is stated in v. 6, "whoever sows sparingly will also reap sparingly, and whoever sows bountifully will also reap bountifully." I will receive based on the way that I give. The second part is stated in v. 7, "Each one must give as he has decided in his heart, not reluctantly or under compulsion, for God loves a cheerful giver." I must purpose ahead of time to give so that I will give cheerfully. The third part is stated in v. 8, "God is able to make all grace abound to you, so that having all sufficiency in all things at all times, you may abound in every good work." God will take care of me if I am a giving person.

Finally, proper giving glorifies God (2 Corinthians 9:12-13).

QUESTIONS TO ASK ABOUT YOUR GIVING

When should I give? First Corinthians 16:1-2 helps us with this question. "Now concerning the collection for the saints: as I directed the churches of Galatia, so you also are to do. On the first day of every week, each of you is to put something aside and store it up, as he may prosper, so that there will be no collecting when I come."

There are two types of giving in the New Testament. The giving in Acts 2-3 was urgent and immediate giving. When the immediate need arose, they gathered up what they needed to alleviate the situation. The giving in 1 Corinthians 16:1-2 is future giving. They were going to be sending to a need at a certain, future time. Therefore, they were instructed to give toward that need on the first day of every week (Sunday) until that time came.

The church operates on these principles today. There are many needs that arise on an emergency basis. At that time, funds are gathered to meet that need. However, there are ongoing, future needs that we know we must meet. For these, we gather funds on the first day of every week.

How much should I give? The New Testament does not say anything about a specific amount to give. The people of the Old Testament were commanded to give specific amounts, but God changed things in the New Testament. First Corinthians 16:2 says to "put something aside." This "something" is based on how I have been prospered from the last time that I gave until the present one.

God left me the freedom to determine how much I will give. Those who demand a "tithe" are pulling something out of the Old Testament and bringing it into the New Testament. The New Testament does not teach "tithing" as the giving standard.

The context of 2 Corinthians 8:1-9:15 provides these ideas when I determine how much and how to give.

I should give willingly (8:3, 12). I should give according to my ability to give, even sacrificially (8:3). I should give bountifully (9:6). I should give purposefully (9:7). I should give cheerfully (9:7). I should give liberally (9:11). If I am giving in this way, then what I give is accepted by God. Giving this way makes me a proper giver.

Why should I give? It is clear that God expects His people to be giving people. God expects me to give. If I do not give, I am dishonoring and disobeying God. However, there are many more reasons to give than simply obeying a commandment of God.

I should give because I love God. God is a giver (John 3:16). His gift of love should motivate me to be a giver. I should give because I love the Church that He established through Jesus. The Church is God's arm in the world to influence and help people. If the Church does not carry out the mission of God, then it will fail. If the members of the church do not support the church financially, the church will not be able to carry out its mission.

I should give because I want to support the work of the church that I am a part of. Each person should be involved in supporting the on-going work of the church. The church is a support for my spiritual life and I should give so that it will continue for me and for others.

I should give because giving helps me to be free from greed.

Those whose hearts are set on having and controlling money are susceptible to the greedy mindset. First Timothy 6:10 sounds this warning, "For the love of money is a root of all kinds of evils. It is through this craving that some have wandered away from the faith and pierced themselves with many pangs." Rather than loving money, which is obviously condemned, Christians should love God and show that love for God through their giving.

REVIEW QUESTIONS

1. "Where your treasure is _____
   _____."

2. Money is a good barometer of our _____.

3. Where does proper giving start?

4. Why were the Macedonians good examples of giving?

5. What was the goal of first century giving in the Church?

6. Proper giving is a reflection of _____
    _____.

7. What are the three parts to the giving principle?

8. When should I give?

9. How much should I give?

10. Why should I give?

11. Is "tithing" a part of New Testament worship?

10

WORSHIP: PRAYER

Prayer is a powerful part of the corporate and personal worship experience. And yet, it may be one of the toughest things for some Christians to do and do well. The disciples of Jesus even had this same problem. Luke 11:1 records that they approached Jesus and said, "Lord, teach us to pray, as John taught his disciples."

Jesus responded with a sample prayer from which He expected them to learn the basic principles of proper prayer. The opening words teach that proper prayer is a form of worship, "Father, hallowed be your name" (Luke 11:2). It is important, then, that we learn what God wants us to know about prayer. We need to learn to pray.

PRAYER PRINCIPLES

The particulars of prayer are important. Prayer is not for informing God about anything. God already knows everything. Therefore, there is nothing that He does not know. Prayer serves to remind us of our position before Him while we utter these thoughts.

The phrase, "Give us each day our daily bread" (Luke 11:3), reminds us that even our daily food is from God. The words, "Forgive us our sins, for we ourselves forgive everyone who is indebted to us" (Luke 11:4), remind us of the importance of forgiving in order to be forgiven. And, the statement, "Lead us not into temptation" (Luke 11:4), reminds us that God is available to help us with the temptations of life.

The purposes in prayer are important. There are at least six purposes in prayer that can be identified in Scripture.

Prayer is supplication. Ephesians 6:18 states, "Praying at all times in the Spirit, with all prayer and supplication. To that end keep alert with all perseverance, making supplication for all the saints." Supplication is pleading.

Prayer should include petition. Matthew 6:11 reads, "Give us this day our daily bread." Petitions are requests of God for things related to daily life. They are expressions of our desires and needs.

Prayer should include thanksgiving. Paul instructed the Thessalonians, "Pray without ceasing, give thanks in all circumstances; for this is the will of God in Christ Jesus for you" (I Thessalonians 5:17-18).

Prayer should include confession. James 5:16 declares, "Confess your sins to one another and pray for one another, that you may be healed. The prayer of a righteous person has great power as it is working."

Prayer should include praise. The words in Jesus' sample prayer, "Hallowed be your name" are words of praise directed toward God. It is not the case that every prayer should contain every one of these things. However, it is true that our prayer lives should include all of these from time to time. They are all important in our relationship with our heavenly Father.

There is a final key point about prayer. James 1:5-8 teaches us about faith and prayer. "If any of you lacks wisdom, let him ask God, who gives generously to all without reproach, and it will be given him. But let him ask in faith, with no doubting, for the one who doubts is like a wave of the sea that is driven and tossed by the wind. For that person must not suppose that he will receive anything from the Lord; he is a double-minded man, unstable in all his ways."

Faith is the attitude that allows prayer to be answered. One who prays without faith chokes off the possibility that the prayer actually will produce anything.

PRINCIPLES FOR PRAYER LEADERS

Public prayer is the time when the gathered group approaches the throne room of God together. There are many texts that show assembled Christians praying together (Acts 1:14; 4:24, 31; 12:5, 12). Those who lead public prayers have an awesome task as they are speaking to God for the gathered group. It is important to observe some helpful principles in order for prayer to be something other than a time-filler.

Avoid personal references. Public prayers during public gatherings of worship are for the group. Therefore, it is better to leave out personal references and pray for things that are on the minds and hearts of the group. Praying about personal sin or personal goals does not speak for the entire group. But the leader's personal life is probably not much different from the rest of the group. So just use group language to speak about personal things because those in the group are probably facing the same things.

Avoid pet phrases. Those who lead public prayers have learned to do so from listening to those who lead. That has led to the continued use of phrases that, though not improper, might better be avoided. Such phrases include: "guide, guard, and direct us; bring us back at the next appointed time; help the speaker to have a ready recollection of what he has studied." Jesus told His disciples, "Do not heap up empty phrases" (Matthew 6:7). His warning was to avoid using words that did not have understood meanings and were used just to fill the space.

Avoid preaching. There certainly is nothing wrong with preaching, but a time of prayer is not primarily a time of teaching. Sure, there is some teaching that comes across, but that is not the focus. The time in worship when public prayers are worded is not the time to quote passages of Scripture. It is not the time to reprimand inappropriate or sinful activity. Prayer is the time when we approach the throne of God. We come before Him in gratitude and humility as we beseech Him in behalf of things in this life. We should give that time our best effort and our fully engaged mind.

REVIEW QUESTIONS

1. What did Jesus' disciples ask Him about prayer in Luke 11:1?

2. Prayer is not for _____.

3. What are the six purposes in prayer?

4. What is the proper attitude in prayer?

11

WORSHIP: PREACHING

A two-way mirror is a valuable tool in criminal investigations. Using this tool, investigators are able to conduct an interview of a suspect, while other officers watch from the other side. They not only get to hear what he says, but also to "see" what he says with his body language.

James 1:21-25 refers to the Bible as a two-way mirror. As I look into the Bible, I see both who I am and who I ought to be. Both scenarios are necessary. I need to appreciate who and what I really am so that I can more readily adapt to who and what I ought to be.

It is the Bible, the Word of God, that is the basis for all we do in life. Our worship must be guided by the authority of the Word. This undergirds all that we do in worship. The "five acts of worship" have been a part of our training from the time that we were children. I know that I learned to use the five fingers on one hand to identify the acts of worship and the five fingers on the other hand to identify the five steps to salvation.

The inherent danger in such a process is to miss the spirit while enumerating the truth. There is a danger in both cases of developing a "checklist mentality." This approach might convince a person that all that is needed is check off the appropriate box after having completed the specific act and think, "What a spiritually-minded person I am!"

We don't really believe such a thing, but we often act as though we do. Therefore, it is important to understand what is behind every step we take toward salvation and what is behind every action we do as we worship God.

SCRIPTURE IS IMPORTANT IN WORSHIP

It may be that we have relegated the word to a lesser role in worship than it deserves or than God desires. We can always do a better job making Scripture more front and center in our singing, at the Lord's Supper, in giving, in prayer, and certainly in preaching.

Notice what Paul wrote to Timothy about this very topic. "Until I come, devote yourself to the public reading of Scripture, to exhortation, to teaching" (1 Timothy 4:13) Each of these charges rests directly on the Word. It was important for Timothy to read the Word so that he could exhort and teach the brethren. Isn't that what preaching is about?

In the previous chapter, Paul wrote what seems to be the theme of the entire book, "I hope to come to you soon, but I am writing these things to you so that, if I delay, you may know how one ought to behave in the household of God, which is the church of the living God, a pillar and buttress of the truth" (1 Timothy 3:14-15).

Paul's instructions addressed Timothy and his participation in a local church setting. The majority of the book addresses aspects of the assembled, worshipping church. Chapter 2 addresses men and women and their participation in the assembly of a local congregation. He specified that the men should take the lead in public prayers. Women are told not to assume any authoritative, leadership role over men in worship or Bible teaching.

Chapter 3 addresses the qualifications of the men who shepherd the flock and those men who carry out the day-to-day functions of the work of the church (deacons). Chapter 4 addresses Timothy in his ministry in behalf of the church as a preacher. Chapter 5 address-es the members of the church and the way that they should treat each other. Chapter 6 addresses those who would teach other doc-trines and how they should be handled. He closes charging Timothy to "guard the deposit entrusted to you"(6:20).

WHAT IS WORSHIP?

The text of John 4:21-24 provides the context from which eight characteristics of worship can be enumerated. The context is Jesus' address to the Samaritan woman at Jacob's well as they engaged a discussion about worship.

Worship is momentary. It begins and it ends. It is not continuous activity. Jesus addressed those who worship" (v. 24). Paul went to Jeru-salem to worship (Acts 24:11), obviously not worshipping on the way.

Worship is intentional. Again, those "who worship" make a choice to do so. Worship is not an accidental, mindless activity.

Worship is personal. Jesus addressed each one who made the choice to worship. He included all the "worshippers" (v. 23).

Worship is vertical. Jesus twice directed all worshippers to the "Father" (v. 23) and once to "God" (v. 24).

Worship is internal. It must be done "in spirit" (v. 24). This in-struction teaches that worship is in the Spirit who has been given to each person by God at the point of baptism.

Worship is structured. It has been ordered by God. Jesus referred to the "true worshippers" (v. 23) and worship in "truth" (v. 24).

Worship is responsive. Worship flows from those who acknowledge that "the Father is seeking such to worship him" (v. 23).

Worship is necessary. "Those who worship him must worship in spirit and truth" (v. 24). There is no choice. God demands that we worship Him.

PREACHING IS WORSHIP

So is preaching a form of worship? It is not worship if it does not convey proper doctrine. There were preachers in Paul's day who taught the wrong doctrine. "But thanks be to God, that you who were once slaves of sin have become obedient from the heart to the standard of teaching to which you were committed, and, having been set free from sin, have become slaves of righteousness" (Romans 16:17-18).

Improper doctrine cannot be a part of proper worship. Just like singing and prayer, preaching must be consistent with the truth of God's word. Paul warned Timothy that there were many who were going to preach this improper doctrine. "For the time is coming when people will not endure sound teaching, but having itching ears they will accumulate for themselves teachers to suit their own passions, and will turn away from listening to the truth and wander off into myths" (2 Timothy 4:3-4)

It is clear that preaching must be of a certain quality. Paul defined the qualities of proper preaching in Titus 1:9—"He must hold firm to the trustworthy word as taught, so that he may be able to give instruction in sound doctrine and also to rebuke those who contradict it."

To the Colossians, Paul commanded, "And when this letter has been read among you, have it also read in the church of the Laodiceans; and see that you also read the letter from Laodicea" (Colossians 4:16). His message to the Thessalonians was the same, "I put you under oath before the Lord to have this letter read to all the brothers" (1 Thessalonians 5:27). Assemblies of the church in the first century included reading various epistles that circulated among the churches.

Preaching is worship as it presents the word of God fully and accurately. Through this kind of preaching, God is glorified. This is worship. The Psalmist expressed the attitude of worship through a study of God's word in his extensive 119th Psalm.

- "I will praise you with an upright heart, when I learn your righteous rules" (v. 7).

- "With my lips I declare all the rules of your mouth. In the way of your testimonies I delight as much as in all riches" (vv. 13-14).

- "Open my eyes, that I may behold wondrous things out of your law" (v. 18).

- "At midnight I rise to praise you, because of your righteous rules" (v. 62).

- "I love your testimonies" (v. 119).

- "Your testimonies are wonderful; therefore my soul keeps them" (v. 129).

- "Righteous are you, O LORD, and right are your rules" (v. 137).

- "My heart stands in awe of your words" (v. 161).

- "Seven times a day I praise you for your righteous rules" (v. 164).

It is the study of the word that is the avenue of worship in preaching. The preacher is but the facilitator of worship. The preacher does not worship more than everyone else in the assembly. Those who lead in worship are facilitators for worship. Song leaders worship God as they lead the assembly in worship through song. Those who pray audibly in the assembly are worshipping God as they pray and the assembly is worshipping God as they pray silently with the one who is leading. Those who stand and serve at the observance of the Lord's Supper and at the collection of freewill offerings of money are facilitating the worship of the assembly making it possible for all to worship through these actions "decently and in order" (1 Corinthians 14:40).

Preaching pays homage to God through a study of His word. Singing pays homage to God as we utter words of praise to Him. Prayer pays homage to God as we express our appreciation for His benefits and ask for His help within His will. The Lord's Supper pays homage to God as we remember the sacrifice paid for our redemption. When we give of our money, we pay homage to God offering back to Him of what He has freely given to us.

Just like the other four ways that God has given His authority for our worship of Him, preaching accomplishes the same purposes and does the same thing. Strong, accurate, clear Bible teaching focuses our minds and hearts on the will of God and appreciates Him for His message teaching us about our salvation.

REVIEW QUESTIONS

1. How is the Bible like a two-way mirror?

2. Why is the "checklist" mentality dangerous?

3. Why is Scripture important in worship?

4. What are the eight words used to define worship in John 4?

5. How is preaching worship?

12.

PERSONAL INVOLVEMENT

The Church belongs to Jesus (Matthew 16:18). He purchased it with His own blood (Ephesians 5:25, 32). It is a bought and paid for institution over which He is the Head (Ephesians 1:22-23). But, the local congregation and assembly of Jesus' Church is my church. I have a personal stake in its existence and in its success. I support it with my treasures, my time, and my talents. Without this kind of support from each member, the local church will not function and survive. Personal involvement is a must!

I AM THE CHURCH

The Church is not the building where Christians assemble. Jesus did not die for a building! The Church is the people. Saul was a persecutor of the Church. "But Saul was ravaging the church, and entering house after house, he dragged off men and women and committed them to prison" (Acts 8:3). He persecuted the Church when he persecuted the people because the people are the Church.

Paul closed the epistle to the Romans with many personal greetings. One greeting was to Aquila and Priscilla (Romans 16:3). Then, he said, "Greet also the church in their house" (Romans 16:5). In 1 Corinthians 11:18, Paul uses the phrase, "when you come together as a church." He then went on to handle some problems the church was experiencing. The church had the problem because the people were at odds with each other.

These verses show that the Christians are the Church. In the Bible, there is no special significance given to any building. And, there is no place where the room or building in which the Christians assembled was ever called a sanctuary. The people who are God's people are holy and sanctified. But the building where they meet is not holy or sanctified.

I AM A PART OF THE CHURCH

The Church is a body made up of many parts, "the body is one and has many members" (1 Corinthians 12:12a). But it is still a body, "all the members of the body, though many, are one body" (1 Corinthians 12:12b). The body figure means that the Church functions as a unit. Therefore, everyone has a part.

The Church is the bride of Christ (2 Corinthians 11:2; Ephesians 5:25-27, 32). The bride figure means that a commitment is necessary in order to be a part. The Church is the family of God (Galatians 2:26-29). The family figure means that a birth is necessary in order to be a part. The Church is the flock of God (Acts 20:28; 1 Peter 5:2). The flock figure shows that faithfulness is necessary in order to remain a part.

I am a part of the body because I have put on Christ in baptism (Galatians 3:26-27). At the same time, I was added to the number of all those who also have been baptized into Christ (Acts 2:47). I am a part with all the other parts.

I NEED TO BE AN ACTIVE PART OF THE CHURCH

Each member has a functional part or role to fulfill if the body is to operate to its fullest potential. To the degree that any one member fails to function, to that same degree the entire church fails to function as well as it could. Each person helps the church be successful.

Each member has talents and abilities to contribute to the work of the church. "For as in one body we have many members, and the members do not all have the same function, so we, though many, are one body in Christ, and individually members one of another" (Romans 12:4-5).

There are so many roles that God needs us to fill in His Church. He needs ambassadors who will represent Him before the world (2 Corinthians 5:20). He needs bakers who will add the leavening of God's Kingdom to the world (Matthew 13:33).

He needs fishermen who will help bring people into the Church (Matthew 4:19). He needs guards who will stand in behalf of His word (1 Timothy 6:20). He needs harvesters who follow up with those in whom the seed has been planted and are ready to bear fruit (Matthew 9:38).

He needs soldiers who will fight the good fight of faith and endure hardships (I Timothy 6:12; II Timothy 2:3). He needs watchmen who will live soberly (I Thessalonians 5:6). He needs wrestlers who will wrestle against the forces of the devil (Ephesians 6:12).

There are also many specific things that need to be done in the work of any local church. Bible teaching, visiting, organization, and communication are just a few of them. And this doesn't even mention the opportunities to serve people. (It would be a good idea at this point to find out the different work areas for the church where you are. You can look through that list and see what you can do. Then, volunteer! Don't wait for someone to come to you!)

BUT SOME OFFER EXCUSES

Paul wrote to the Corinthian church to answer questions about things happening among them (1 Corinthians 1:11; 7:1). In chapter 12, he dealt with those who offer excuses for not being an active part of the body. Verse 14 records, "For the body does not consist of one member but of many." A body, by definition, has many functioning parts that help it to work properly and well.

Verses 15-16 deal with excuse-making. "If the foot should say, 'Because I am not a hand, I do not belong to the body,' that would not make it any less a part of the body. And if the ear should say, 'Because I am not an eye, I do not belong to the body,' that would not make it any less a part of the body." There are four excuses in these verses. These are excuses that any of us might be tempted to use from time to time.

The first excuse is, "I'm not important." Those who use this excuse have a low opinion of themselves. In Paul's analogy, the foot and the ear do not think they are as important as they actually are.

The second excuse is, "I'm not as important as others." Those who use this excuse have a low opinion of themselves as compared to others. In the text, the foot thinks it is not as important as the hand. The ear thinks it is not as important as the eye.

The third excuse is, "I don't have as prominent a position as I want." Those who use this excuse want recognition for their work that they think they are not getting in their current position. That's the problem the foot has. It thinks that it is not getting as much credit as the hand. After all, the foot is constantly being stepped on by the rest of the body, and it smells all the time! The foot's assessment of its situation is that, since its position is not as prominent as the hand, it is not really a part of the body.

The fourth excuse is, "I don't have as good a job as I want." Those who use this excuse devalue the contribution they make to the body. That's the problem with the ear. It thinks its job is of such less value than the job of the eye that it believes it is not really a part of the body. "Since I am not that part, I am not a part!"

The assessment of the situation by the foot and the ear is ludicrous. They certainly are important parts in the body. That's the conclusion Paul makes in v. 17, "If the whole body were an eye, where would be the sense of hearing? If the whole body were an ear, where would be the sense of smell?"

Both the foot and the ear had the problem of stinkin' thinkin'. They gave in to the notion that there are some jobs and positions that are so much better than others that the less important jobs would not even be missed. But, would any body volunteer to give up its ears? Would any body volunteer to give up its feet? The notion is incredible!

Verse 21, however, warns those members who seem to be more honorable that every part of the body is important. "The eye cannot say to the hand, "I have no need of you," nor again the head to the feet, 'I have no need of you.'"

The truth is that those parts of the body that receive less attention and are not as noticeable are extremely important. When was the last time you sat down and contemplated your kidneys? Or, when did you last take stock of your spleen?

We do not think very much about these body parts until something goes wrong with them and, then, everything stops in order to care for them. This is exactly what Paul says in vv. 22-25.

"On the contrary, the parts of the body that seem to be weaker are indispensable, and on those parts of the body that we think less honorable we bestow the greater honor, and our unpresentable parts are treated with greater modesty, which our more presentable parts do not require. But God has so composed the body, giving greater honor to the part that lacked it, that there may be no division in the body, but that the members may have the same care for one another."

No one should hide behind any excuse and fail to be involved in the work of the Church. Every single person has something to contribute to a local congregation. All they need is some help discovering what that is and an opportunity to put it into service. No church can survive without involvement from its members. After all, that's what the church is—the people!

REVIEW QUESTIONS

1. The Church belongs to _____.

2. What is the Church?

3. Does the building have a sanctuary?

4. The Church is described by what figures?

5. All members should _____ for service.

6. What are the four excuses the various parts made in 1 Corinthians 12?

13

THE ROLE OF WOMEN

There are many "hot-button" issues that continue to stir questions and foster debate. The issue of the role of women in the leadership of the Church is surely one of the hottest. The heat comes often from a false belief that those who teach a limited role of women in leadership, generally, have less than a Christian attitude toward women. Admittedly, someone might be able to level an accurate charge that we have not used women in the work of the Church as fully as we should. But, it is not fair to say that teaching a limited role for women in worship and Bible teaching is not a Christian attitude.

WOMEN: BE SILENT

The principal passage for this study is 1 Timothy 2:8-15. In this text, Paul emphasizes the need for women to be concerned about modesty. He says that they should "adorn themselves in respectable apparel, with modesty and self-control, not with braided hair and gold or pearls or costly attire, but with what is proper for women who profess godliness—with good works" (vv. 9-10). Godly women do not draw attention to themselves through expensive clothing or jewelry. They want to be known for their godliness through their good works.

Having addressed dress, Paul now turns to demeanor. How should they conduct themselves? "Let a woman learn quietly with all submissiveness. I do not permit a woman to teach or to exercise authority over a man; rather, she is to remain quiet" (vv. 11-12).

It is obvious that this discussion is about those times when men and women are together. It is, also, obvious that this is a time when they are together in a situation where Bible teaching is taking place. This text is not addressing the secular work world.

And the text is not addressing a worship assembly exclusively. It is addressing any situation where Bible teaching is taking place. The first thing Paul says to the women is, "Be quiet! " The Greek word is *hasuchia*. *Thayer's Greek-English Lexicon of the New Testament* gives this definition: "quietness; descriptive of the life of one who stays at home doing his own work, and does not officiously meddle with the affairs of others." The word, then, does not tell women to be quiet and not say anything. It refers to the quiet demeanor with which a woman conducts herself while saying something or while saying nothing.

The Greek word *sigao* is the word that means "to be quiet; hold one's peace." It means not to say anything or hush. This word is used in 1 Corinthians 14:34 where Paul tells the women who possess the miraculous gifts of tongue-speaking and prophesying not to use them in the assembly of the Church. In other words, "Hush!"

The word "silence" used in 1 Timothy 2:11 should be understood with the word "submission." Women are supposed to learn with a submissive demeanor in quietness. The verse teaches a woman to speak with a proper demeanor.

Verse 12 limits a woman's speaking. Paul said, "I do not permit..." This is a forceful statement. The word "permit" is used in many other places in the New Testament. In every case, it carries the idea that someone has authority and someone is under that authority. Whatever the authority permits, the other takes as license or permission.

One of the best illustrations of this is the incident of Jesus casting the demons out of a man who was so controlled by them that he had superhuman strength and was not in his right mind (Luke 8). The demons begged Jesus to "permit" them to enter into a herd of pigs. The text continues, "And He permitted them. " (v. 32 NKJV) Jesus was the authority and the demons were under that authority and were subject to it.

So, what is the authoritative message from Paul on this topic? A woman is not "to teach or to exercise authority over a man" (1 Timothy 2:12) Again, the point is not that she cannot teach a man. It is that she cannot teach over a man. She cannot possess an authoritative role over men in the preaching and teaching of God's word. Certainly, women may teach God's word, even to men. They do this while singing in the worship assembly for instance (Ephesians 5:19; Colossians 3:16). That same Greek word for "silence" appears at the end of v. 12. A woman is to "remain silent." She may teach with quietness. She may not teach in the same authoritative way that men should.

Paul, then, clarifies his message even more. He gives two reasons why we are to follow this edict. "For Adam was formed first, then Eve; and Adam was not deceived, but the woman was deceived and became a transgressor" (vv. 13-14).

It was not culture that produced this instruction. It was creation. The creation order was Adam first, then Eve. Neither was it a value judgment between men and women that spurred this instruction. Men are not more valuable than women. Both the man and the woman whom God placed in the Garden of Eden sinned.

There was a difference, however, between the two of them in

their sins. Eve sinned by deception. Adam sinned by decision. He knew the penalty for violating God's instruction (Genesis 2:16-17) and he chose that penalty (death) over losing his wife (because he knew that by eating she was going to die). For these two reasons and no more, God placed these restrictions on women as pertains to the teaching and preaching of God's word.

Further proof for this position lies in v. 8, "I desire then that in every place the men should pray, lifting holy hands without anger or quarreling." There are two different words translated "men" or "man" in vv. 1-8. The word *anthropos* appears in vv. 1, 4, and 5. This word means "mankind," including both men and women.

The other Greek word *aner* appears in vv. 5, 8. This word means "men" as opposed to women. Those who read the original letter from Paul knew immediately that he was making a distinction between mankind and men.

We should pray for all mankind (v. 1). God wants all mankind to be saved (v. 4). And, Jesus is the Mediator between God and all mankind (v. 5). But, Jesus was a man and not a woman (v. 5). And men—not women—are to pray (vocally and publicly) when both men and women are assembled together (v. 8). There is no authority from this passage for women to have an authoritative role over men either in teaching God's word or verbalizing prayers in mixed assemblies.

WOMEN: BE SUBMISSIVE

The word *submission* carries such negative connotations that whenever the subject is discussed the tension in the room is tenable. *Thayer's Greek-English Lexicon of the New Testament* defines this word, "to arrange under, to subordinate; to subject, put in subjection." It is used 33 times in the New Testament.

General submission of both men and women is a fact of life. "But I want you to understand that the head of every man is Christ, the head of a wife is her husband, and the head of Christ is God" (1 Corinthians 11:3). Paul even admonished that all of us should be "submitting to one another out of reverence for Christ" (Ephesians 5:21). Therefore, neither men nor women can claim to be exempt from the submissive principle. Even Jesus, while on the earth, was submissive to the will of the Father (John 5:30).

But there is also special submission. It is in this discussion that most of the trouble over the issue arises. However, not all arenas of special submission produce the same amount of heat. We must be submissive to the government (Romans 13:1-7; 1 Peter 2:13-17). Children must be submissive to their parents (Ephesians 6:1-2). Employees must be submissive to their employers (Ephesians 6:5-8). Even employers are to be submissive to the will of God and treat their employees well (Ephesians 6:9). We certainly know that the Church is to be submissive to the shepherds who care for her (Hebrews 13:17). None of these areas generate as much heat as the discussion of the special submission of women.

Women must be submissive to their husbands at home (Ephesians 5:22-33). And they must be submissive to the men in the assembly and in Bible teaching (1 Timothy 2:9-15). But the subject of submission should not be an oppressive burden. God, Himself, defines what this word means.

Men and women are equal in the sight of God. Special submission does not take away from this any more than Jesus' submission to His Father took anything away from His equality to God (John 6:38; 8:29; 16:28; Philippians 2:6; Hebrews 1:3; 5:8).

Submission is not a weapon to be used against those who are to be in submission. There is no place in Scripture where men are given permission to put women in submission. Women must give that of their own free will. There is no place in Scripture where God forces our submission to Him. God wants us to give Him our submission of our own free will.

Yes, women may very well be the most underused group in any local church. They are a wealth of energy and creative talent that can help any church grow and be a valuable asset to God. The stories of Dorcas (Acts 9:36-43), Lois and Eunice (Acts 16:1-4; 2 Timothy 1:5; 3:14-15; 1 Peter 3:1-2), Lydia (Acts 16:11-15), Phoebe (Romans 16:1-2), Priscilla (Romans 16:3-4; Acts 18:2-28), and many others show the value of women to the Lord. Also, consider the instructions to women about their roles of leadership in their own special ways (Titus 2:3-5; 1 Timothy 5:3-14). There can be no doubt that women are valuable before God and have valuable leadership qualities.

However, this is not proof that women have the authority from God to preach, serve as elders or deacons, or serve in whatever way the men are serving. God has defined the roles for men and women as He desires. It is our job to comply with His wishes.

REVIEW QUESTIONS

1. What is the definition of submission?

2. What did Paul mean when he told women to be quiet in 1 Timothy 2?

3. What did Paul mean when he told women to be quiet in 1 Corinthians 14?

4. What two reasons are given in 1 Timothy 2 for women not having authority?

5. Eve sinned by _____.

6. Adam sinned by _____.

7. What two words are translated "man" in 1 Timothy 2?

8. How are these two words different?

9. Do men have authority to put women in submission?

PERSONAL NOTES

PERSONAL NOTES

PERSONAL NOTES

PERSONAL NOTES

PERSONAL NOTES

PERSONAL NOTES

PERSONAL NOTES

PERSONAL NOTES

PERSONAL NOTES

PERSONAL NOTES

PERSONAL NOTES

PERSONAL NOTES

PERSONAL NOTES

To order additional Bible Studies from Start2Finish,
visit start2finish.org/bible-studies, call (888) 978-3850,
or ask for them at your favorite Christian bookstore.

Also available for Kindle, Nook, & iBooks.

www.ingramcontent.com/pod-product-compliance
Lightning Source LLC
Chambersburg PA
CBHW061148040426
42445CB00013B/1615